# CONTENTS

# LIGHT of LIGHTS

ADVENT DEVOTIONS FROM

## THE UPPER ROOM

DAILY DEVOTIONAL GUIDE

UPPER
ROOM BOOKS®
NASHVILLE

LIGHT OF LIGHTS
Advent Devotions from *The Upper Room* daily devotional guide
© 2014 by Upper Room Books. All rights reserved.

The Upper Room® website http://www.upperroom.org

Cover and interior design: Bruce Gore / gorestudio.com

Library of Congress Cataloging-in-Publication Data

Light of lights : Advent devotions from the Upper Room daily devotional guide.
    pages cm
  Includes bibliographical references and index.
  ISBN 978-0-8358-1341-9 (print : alk. paper) — ISBN 978-0-8358-1342-6 (mobi) —
ISBN 978-0-8358-1343-3 (epub)
1. Advent--Prayers and devotions.
  BV40.L55 2014
  242'.332--dc23
                              2013049536

Printed in the United States of America

# INTRODUCTION

*Come, draw us in, hold us together*
*while we wait for the birth of the Light of lights,*
*the One who will guide us into the world anew. Amen.*
—PAMELA C. HAWKINS

We begin this Advent season with prayerful and hopeful hearts. Advent invites us to commit to daily prayer practice, to be attentive to where God is present in our lives, to look for the light. This book will guide and encourage you to journey through Advent with a focus on the coming of Christ. You may read this book individually, with your family, or with a group that gathers weekly to discuss it and pray together.

Each week's theme is patterned after the traditional Advent wreath with the candles representing Hope, Love, Joy and Peace. A fifth week includes meditations for Christmas Eve, Christmas Day, and the Sunday after Christmas. Each of the weeks of Advent includes six meditations to read Monday through Saturday. Sunday is reserved for the small-group gathering. A complete Advent Small-Group Guide is found at the back of this book.

Read the meditation for each day, slowly and prayerfully. Read the suggested scripture and spend some time with the reflection question, journaling your thoughts, if you like. Making notes will help you remember some discussion points for your weekly group gathering.

## ABOUT ADVENT

Advent is a season of four weeks that includes the four Sundays before Christmas. Advent derives from the Latin *adventus*, which means "coming." The season proclaims the coming of the Christ—whose birth we prepare to celebrate once again.

## ABOUT THE ADVENT WREATH

Whether you are studying the book alone, with your family, or with a small group, you will find the ritual of lighting the candles on an Advent wreath each week to be a tangible way to mark the passing of the season. You can buy an Advent wreath at many department stores or online, but a less expensive option is to make your own. Following this introduction are simple instructions for making an Advent wreath.

The Advent wreath—four candles on a wreath of evergreen—is shaped in a circle to symbolize the eternity of God. In some churches, four purple candles, one for each week in Advent, are used with one larger white candle in the middle as the Christ candle. Other churches prefer three purple or blue candles with one candle being rose or pink, to represent joy, with the white Christ candle in the middle.

The lighting of the first candle symbolizes hope, the second symbolizes love, the third joy, and the fourth peace. The Christ candle is lit on Christmas Eve or Christmas Day, reminding us that Jesus is the light of the world. The Advent Small-Group Guide includes prayers to say with the lighting of each candle.

May these meditations encourage and challenge you as you wait for the coming of Christ, the Light of lights.

# HOW TO MAKE AN ADVENT WREATH

## Materials

Flame-retardant artificial evergreen wreath
3   Purple taper candles
1   Pink or rose-colored taper candle
1   Tall white pillar candle
Floral candleholders (4 taper and 1 pillar,
available at craft stores)
Decorations for wreath, such as small artificial
pinecones or berries
Wire or floral sticks

## Instructions

1. Place wreath flat on a table.
2. Evenly space four candles—three purple and one rose.
3. Attach the candles with floral candleholders.
4. Place white pillar candle into a candleholder, and set it in the center of the wreath.
5. Decorate the wreath with pinecones, berries, or anything you like. Use wire or floral sticks to attach them to the wreath.

## Lighting the Candles

On the first Sunday of Advent, which is the fourth Sunday before Christmas, light one of the purple candles. This candle represents the hope that the coming of Christ brings to the world.

On the next Sunday of Advent, light two candles—first, the candle from the previous week, and then another purple candle. This candle represents the love of God, demonstrated by sending Christ into the world.

On the third Sunday of Advent, light three candles—the previous two candles in the order they were originally lit, then the rose-colored candle, which represents the joy of anticipating the coming of Christ.

On the fourth Sunday of Advent, the previous three candles are lit in order, plus the final purple candle, which represents the peace Christ brings to the world.

On Christmas Day or the Sunday after Christmas, all five candles are lit in order, including the white one in the center, to celebrate the arrival of Christ.

# FIRST WEEK OF ADVENT

*Hope*

## INTRODUCTION

*Could it be that my aching for the anguish of the world*
*Is the feeling of my heart being enlarged?*
*Could it be that my willingness to ache for my suffering neighbor*
*Is my purest assent to God's perfect intent?*

—ROBERT CARR

In the season of Advent, we are called to share the hope that we have in Christ with a hope-famished world. In the meditations for this week, we are challenged and encouraged to

- open our eyes and look for Christ with the eyes of a child.
- open our ears and listen for the sounds of hope in this season.
- lean toward the light, even when our circumstances are dismal.
- offer hope to the hurting among us.
- wait in solidarity with the poor and the suffering.
- hang on, despite all the fear that may be swirling around us.

Prepare your heart to be open to this season before you, a season full of sights and sounds and needs. Commit to setting aside a brief time every day to read the scripture and meditation for the day. Pause and breathe. God is near.

## *Looking for Jesus*

**READ JOHN 1:35–41**

An angel . . . appeared to them, and the glory of the Lord shone around them, and they were terrified. . . . When they had seen [the baby], they spread the word concerning what had been told them about this child. —LUKE 2:9, 17 (NIV)

As my wife and I walked from the church with our four-year-old son, we saw a heavily bearded man approaching us. I had seen the man before and was familiar with his fast-paced gait but had not noticed him more than to exchange occasional greetings. Upon seeing the man, my son shouted, "Daddy, see Jesus coming right in front of us!"

Apparently, my son's image of Jesus came from the children's Bible storybooks and movies that depict Jesus as a heavily bearded, light-skinned man. As I chuckled, I remembered the shepherds who were watching over their flocks on the night Christ was born and how startled and frightened they had been. Reflecting on this, I admired my son's excitement at seeing and meeting "Jesus" that day.

As we approach this Christmas, my son's exclamation reminds me to look for Jesus. When we focus on Christ instead of allowing ourselves to be distracted by the many interruptions we encounter every day, we are able to spread the word about his birth and saving grace for all people!

—**Philip Polo (Nairobi, Kenya)**

### *Reflection Question*
How am I looking for Jesus this Advent season?

### *Prayer*
God of all seasons, as we commemorate your son's birth give us child-like awe and enthusiasm for spreading his message of hope. Amen.

# *Hope* · DAY TWO

## *The Sound of Hope*

READ EPHESIANS 3:14-21

Faith is the substance of things hoped for, the evidence of things not seen. —HEBREWS 11:1 (KJV)

Like the tune of a Christmas carol that won't go away, the phrase "the wrong sound weakens" (from a poem by William Stafford) has been coming to my mind again and again. The wrong sound— any word or sound that is out of harmony with God's truth— can only weaken. But a word of truth spoken at the right time, in the right spirit, can change everything about us and about our lives. It's like the clear, pure sound of a trumpet rising above a noisy crowd.

The song the shepherds heard on the first Christmas announcing the good news of the Savior was that sort of sound. Advent reminded us to watch and work for the time when the song of the angels would become the song the whole world sings. We waited for fulfillment of the promise. Sometimes it felt as if the wrong sound would drown out everything else. But then somehow, somewhere deep within, we began to hear the gentle hum that reminds us God is always at work. This hum is what the Bible calls hope.

To believe the gospel is to believe that Jesus Christ is the Word of truth, the Sound who changes everything. Following Christ frees us from the ordinary ways the world conditions us to live and offers us an eternal hope. At Christmas, we come to see that the good news the angels proclaimed is the only sound that can save us.

—James A. Harnish (Florida, USA)

### *Reflection Question*
How do you bring the sound of hope to your world?

### *Prayer*
God of hope, when we are tempted to give up, remind us to listen for the sound of angels. Amen.

# *Hope* · DAY THREE

## *Leaning toward the Light*

**READ JOHN 1:1-5**

The light shines in the darkness, and the darkness did not overcome it. —JOHN 1:5 (NRSV)

When my wife was diagnosed with breast cancer, our initial conversation turned toward the gloom of illness and death. There were tears, fears, and struggles as she grappled with the possibilities that lay before her. But then a light flickered. As she turned her attention toward healing, a light began to grow in the darkness. It grew brighter as people expressed support and prayed for her. This gave us hope. Some people provided books and other information that helped her move from darkness to light.

Her faith in God gave her the assurance that cancer would not have the final word. God's healing would be her light in the darkness. As she recovered over the Advent/Christmas season at home, our family grew closer in love. That holy season took on new meaning. God's love was abundant—everywhere evident in the lights, sounds, and aromas of the season.

As John proclaimed centuries ago, the darkness cannot overcome the light. The light of God is love—a fire, an illumination, a dance—that enables us to trust in our Creator's grace. This light also transforms our dark places into lustrous examples of the power of God.

**Todd Outcalt (Indiana, USA)**

### *Reflection Question*

Do you have a story about how the light of God, perhaps through other people, brought hope to you in a difficult time?

### *Prayer*

God of light, help us to give to you our hard times and our fears. In Jesus' name we pray. Amen.

# *Hope* · DAY FOUR

## *Offering Hope to the Hurting*

**READ PSALM 146**

The king will say, "I was hungry and you gave me food . . . thirsty and you gave me . . . drink, I was a stranger and you welcomed me . . . naked and you gave me clothing . . . sick and you took care of me, I was in prison and you visited me." —MATTHEW 25:35-36 (NRSV)

For three years I have served on the volunteer chaplain staff at a juvenile detention center. Our purpose is to offer troubled youth an opportunity to learn more about our Christian faith and how it can help them in their lives.

During one Christmas service at the center, I was reminded that while I was planning another wonderful Christmas with my family, others were not so fortunate. Yet these young people often disguise their sadness—including their sadness at being in jail at this time of year. Fortunately, we are able to talk with them and pray that the Spirit of God will help us to bring them hope.

Though I am very different from many of these young men, my understanding of Jesus' words in Matthew 25:35-36 reminds me to reach beyond social boundaries. Jesus came to offer hope to those who were suffering. He must have known of the anguish of the imprisoned; he told us to serve all who hurt. The Advent season is the perfect time to offer hope to those who hurt.

**Donald Wallace (Arkansas, USA)**

### *Reflection Question*
What is your practice of offering hope to the needy during this Advent season?

### *Prayer*
Eternal God, help us to be willing to reach out and bring hope to those in need—this Advent season and all year long. Amen.

## *Hope in the Darkness*

READ LUKE 21:25-36

Stand up and raise your heads, because your redemption is drawing near. —LUKE 21:28 (NRSV)

In the season of Advent, we practice waiting for Christ's return. A few years ago, I decided to give up something for Advent so that I could watch and wait for Christ in deeper solidarity with those whose lives are characterized by poverty and suffering sacrifice. I gave up rich foods and desserts until the feast day of Christmas, hoping that my heart might be more open to the presence of Christ. It was a challenging sacrifice, one about which I received regular inquiries, and one that gave me unexpected opportunities to wait actively for Christ.

When suffering, hardship, or disaster come, are we prepared to stand firm and place our hope in the God who has come in Jesus Christ? A South African colleague recently described the experiences of her forebears who lived during the beginning of apartheid. Families were forcibly removed in trucks from their communities and taken into exile to the so-called homelands. Singing arose on those trucks as loving parents comforted their children and offered songs of hope.

In dark times, gifts of memory and hope sustain us, bringing strength to stand in the face of cruel injustice. God grant us the courage to seek justice and peace for all as we wait for the fullness of Christ's coming.

**Diane Luton Blum (Tennessee, USA)**

### *Reflection Question*

How might God be calling you to be in solidarity with those in the world who have no hope?

### *Prayer*

O God, during this season give us eyes to see all around us signs of Christ's love breaking into the world. Amen.

## *Hang On!*

**READ MICAH 5:2-5**

Let the peace of Christ rule in your hearts. —COLOSSIANS 3:15 (NRSV)

About eight hundred years before Jesus was born, a prophet named Micah brought the people of Israel good news. They needed good news. Their country had frequently been attacked by other countries. Armies had marched through Israel, taking over small villages and making slaves of the people. The result was a nation of people who lived in fear. Into this world of pain, Micah spoke a message of hope, telling God's people to hang on and to wait for the salvation God had promised.

Like the people of Israel, many people today live in a state of fear. When we see the bad things that happen in our world, it is easy to become afraid. But the message of Advent is hope. Two promises from Micah's words stand out for me: God's people will live securely, and Christ will be their peace. We can live securely, even in troubled times, as long as our hope rests in God. In his first coming, Christ brought the opportunity for us to experience peace with God. We look forward to his second coming, when all wars will cease and weapons will be destroyed (see Micah 4:3).

**Anne Trudel (Tennessee, USA)**

### *Reflection Question*
In what areas of your life are you being called out of fear and into hope?

### *Prayer*
Dear God, help us to hang on to hope today. Amen.

# SECOND WEEK OF ADVENT
## *Love*

## INTRODUCTION

*God calls us to come home for Christmas. God calls us to come back from all those places where we have settled for less than the fullness of life promised to us in Christ. God calls us back from all the ambitions and possessions we have pursued, thinking they would satisfy us. God calls us to let go of any bitterness and resistance to forgive that block the light of love from warming us. . . . God calls us to come home and to rest, to be embraced by one who loves us as we are. God offers us a place where we are fully known and also fully accepted.*

—MARY LOU REDDING

Many people experience the season of Advent as a time when love is more readily felt, spoken about, and seen in the actions of others. But for others, the season only emphasizes the love and lives that have been lost.

This week we read meditations about opening ourselves up to God's love, coming home to God from all the places we have wandered. We experience the God called *Immanuel*, or "God with us." We picture the God who sings about us and shouts love to us. We remember that God's love often comes to us through the love of others. And we are reminded to give to others in need as an expression of the love we've received.

Your invitation this week is to enjoy God's love and to remember that God takes delight in you. God is calling you to come home for Christmas, a place where you are fully known and accepted.

# *Love* · DAY ONE

## *Are You Ready?*

**READ ISAIAH 40:1-5**

Make straight in the desert a highway for our God. —ISAIAH 40:3
(NRSV)

The other day someone asked me if I was ready for Christmas. My response was, "Ready or not—here it comes!" Advent asks all of us that same question.

Isaiah called people to "make straight" a way for the Lord. The modern equivalent of the prophet's image is heavy earth-movers and dynamite. We prepare for God to come by bulldozing away and washing away all that is unholy. But despite our efforts to be awake and alert, we are often more "not" than "ready." It's like every birth. Parents can never really be prepared for change as radical as the change every baby brings. It's also like every death. We may have had months, even years, to prepare, but when the one we love takes that last breath, it still hits us as if from our blind side. It's like hearing the doctor say, "It's cancer." We've walked that road with others. But when we need others to walk it with us, it's different in a way we cannot get ready for.

Life comes to us whether we're ready or not. There will always be surprises we can't anticipate and demands we can't prepare for. I suspect that's why one of the names of the Holy One is *Immanuel*, which means "God with us." Or, as the Voice of heaven said to the apostle Paul, "My grace is sufficient for you" (2 Cor. 12:9). Faith is trusting that God's grace is and will be enough. That is as ready as we'll ever be.

**Mike Ripski (Tennessee, USA)**

### *Reflection Question*
How does knowing God as *Immanuel*, "God with us," help you to face in life what you can never prepare for?

### *Prayer*
O God, in times when we're ready and times when we're not, help us to trust in and lean on your grace. Amen.

## *God Sings!*

**READ ZEPHANIAH 3:14-20**

[The Lord] will rejoice over you with gladness, he will renew you in his love; he will exult over you with loud singing. —ZEPHANIAH 3:17 (NRSV)

I t is difficult for me to remember that God loves me. I say it with my lips and know it in my head, but I keep forgetting it in my heart. I work hard at being a good person, someone God would be proud of, but like many people, in the midst of my hard work, I forget that God loves me just as I am.

As I was searching for a theme for my personal Advent preparations, this idea kept presenting itself to me. In conversations, music, and words I read, the Holy Spirit kept trying to give me the message that I am loved. It wasn't until I was home sick one day, lazily reading through my Bible, that this message finally got through to me.

When I read Zephaniah 3:17, I pictured God looking down and singing about me. God was singing about the joy of creating me, not about all the things I have done. God's joy comes from loving the creation—me! This is my work for Advent: to enjoy God's love and to remember that God takes delight in me.

**Chris Hlinak (Illinois, USA)**

### *Reflection Questions*
What if your work for Advent were simply to enjoy God's love and God's delight in you? How would that make your Advent experience different?

### *Prayer*
God of joy, forgive us when we forget the most important gift of all— your unconditional love. Help us to remember that you love us so much you sing about it. Amen.

# $\mathscr{Love}$ · DAY THREE

## Love Came Down

**READ MATTHEW 28:16-20**

"They shall name him Emmanuel," which means, "God is with us."
—MATTHEW 1:23 (NRSV)

The first chapter of Matthew tells us Jesus would be called *Emmanuel*, which means "God with us." In the closing chapter, Christ tells us, "Remember, I am with you always, to the end of the age" (28:20). The Gospel ends with the assurance of God's presence.

For my family, last Advent was a bittersweet journey. My fifty-two-year-old brother died after a four-month struggle with cancer. The outpouring of love our family experienced during his illness and in the dark days that followed gave proof of God's faithfulness in being with us. We heard from many friends and relatives who celebrated with us the joy of having known Don and expressed their concern for us in our grief. They were Emmanuel, the powerful presence of God in Jesus Christ made known to us in words and deeds of compassion.

Two thousand years ago, love came to us in the form of the newborn Christ child. Last year, we experienced that love in our home at Christmas through our friends and family. We have no doubt that we were surrounded by Emmanuel then and will be to the end of the age.

**Jean Fitch Justice (Minnesota, USA)**

### Reflection Question
In what form has God's love come to you during this Advent season?

### Prayer
Emmanuel, open our hearts to your love so we may bear good news to those in need this season. Amen.

# $\mathcal{L}ove$ · DAY FOUR

## *A Record of Tears*

### READ ISAIAH **61:1-3**

You know how troubled I am; you have kept a record of my tears.
—PSALM 56:8 (GNT)

$M$y voice faded out as the singing continued around me. Emotion welled up within me. Unwanted tears forced their way out. The words of the song spoke of giving to Jesus our "tears and sadness" and our "years of pain."

Those words broke through my control, and the deep sadness within me welled up. The heartache and hurts of a difficult marriage had built up over many years, and now the final breakup had come. Grief for the loss and failure of many hopes and dreams had been my constant companion for a long time, but I had coped and seemed strong. Yes, I had carried on because of my faith in God's strength. But now it was time to let go. I had to allow my Savior, Jesus Christ, to carry me, enfolded in his love. He knew all about the tears and sadness—how great the pain was and the many years I had borne it.

The advent of Jesus was the fulfillment of the prophecy in Isaiah. Jesus came to bind up the brokenhearted, to comfort those who mourn, and to restore their joy. Grief is a natural response to loss, and though the loss does not go away, I have the wonderful comfort of knowing that Jesus is with me and wants to help bear my sorrow. Not one of our tears falls without his knowing and caring.

**Norma Dawson (New South Wales, Australia)**

### *Reflection Question*
What sadness or pain do you need to release to the love of God?

### *Prayer*
Lord Jesus, thank you for your love and for the comfort of your sustaining presence. Amen.

# $\mathcal{L}ove$ · DAY FIVE

## *A Gift of Warmth*

[Jesus] said to his disciples, " . . . do not worry about your life, what you will eat, or about your body, what you will wear. For life is more than food, and the body more than clothing." —LUKE 12:22-23 (NRSV)

One Christmas when my children were young and I was a single parent attending college, an anonymous donor or donors provided Christmas gifts for my family. Among the gifts was a snowsuit for my three-year-old son, who loved to play in the snow. I remember the first time he came inside after playing in his new snowsuit. As I took off the coat, I could feel the warmth of his body still in the fibers of the coat. I realized that he had never before been so warm while playing out in the snow. Tears came to my eyes as I gave thanks to God for the generosity of those strangers who provided for my little boy.

Now I am in a position to help others who may be struggling to be warm or to eat or to go to school. While Jesus told us not to worry about what we will eat or what we will wear, I know from personal experience that it is easier not to worry when someone comes along to help us in our struggles.

By God's guidance and with God's help, we can help others to live with fewer worries. We can show them by our acts of love and care that God's love is the answer to our worry or fear.

**Susan I. Shelso (Minnesota, USA)**

### *Reflection Question*
How can you give back this Advent season, giving to someone who may be struggling and in need?

### *Prayer*
Dear God, help us to comfort others in their worries as you comfort us. Amen.

## *Shouting Love*

**READ PSALM 33:4-5**

God sent his only Son into the world so that we might live through him. —1 JOHN 4:9 (NRSV)

It was a few days before Christmas. I was to conduct a carol service at a local nursing home. I decided to leave the car in the garage and take my bike. As I mounted the bike, my granddaughter, Bonnie, suddenly shouted, "I love you!"

I called back, "I love you too!"

After I'd gone a few yards, I heard another shout, "Granddad, I love you." As I got to the bottom of the road and much to the amusement of passersby, she yelled at the top of her voice, "I love you, Granddad!"

I cycled on, thinking, *Only a small child would shout in the street, "I love you!"* Then I realized: that is what Christmas is all about—God through Jesus shouting to us, "I love you!"

The heartwarming message of this season is as simple and profound as that. God truly loves us and sent that message through the birth and life of Jesus Christ.

**Peter Bolt (Powys, Wales)**

### *Reflection Question*
Are you more likely to "hear" God's shouts or God's whispers of love?

### *Prayer*
Thank you, God, for sending Jesus to assure us of your love. Amen.

# THIRD WEEK OF ADVENT

## Joy

## INTRODUCTION

*Take time to be aware that in the very midst of our busy preparations for the celebration of Christ's birth in ancient Bethlehem, Christ is reborn in the Bethlehems of our homes and daily lives. Take time, slow down, be still, be awake to the Divine Mystery that looks so common and so ordinary yet is wondrously present.*

—EDWARD HAYS

This week we ponder the elusive concept of joy. We all want to feel it during the Advent season, yet sometimes the more we chase it, the more it flees.

These meditations point us in the direction of true joy

- in family gatherings, even when our expectations are not met.
- by shifting our emphasis, even slightly, from gift-buying to gratitude for the gift of relationships.
- by looking to the eternal for joy rather than temporary fixes.
- by seeing the bigger picture rather than only the circumstances at hand.
- by putting our joy into practice by taking action.
- by focusing on preparing our hearts for the coming of Christ.

As we round this third week toward the coming of the Holy One, may our hearts be called to "come to Christmas," as the last meditation of this week invites us.

# *Joy* · DAY ONE

## *Time Together*

READ ACTS 2:41-47

She gave birth to her firstborn son and wrapped him in bands of cloth, and laid him in a manger, because there was no place for them in the inn. —LUKE 2:7 (NRSV)

My husband had set the table beautifully for a family Advent dinner. The lights were low, music was playing softly, and the Advent wreath the children had made decorated the center of the table.

Not everyone cooperated, however. I let the rice burn in the pan. Our son was more interested in his train than our celebration. Our daughter, tired after not sleeping well, cried through most of the meal. Both children tried to blow out the Advent candle as though it were on a birthday cake.

Our family dinner wasn't the meaningful celebration I had imagined it would be. Did we allow all this to dampen our spirits? No. Many of the activities we plan for our family don't turn out as we hope or expect, but they can still be important times we spend together. Our lives don't always go according to plan. After all, Mary probably didn't intend to have her first child in a stable filled with farm animals.

But we can focus on the love we share and celebrate the time we have together. The presence of God and those we care about can make any event special.

**Nancy A. Johnson (Georgia, USA)**

### *Reflection Question*
How do you experience joy in family settings, even when things don't go as planned?

### *Prayer*
Loving God, help us to find joy in every situation. Let us experience your presence whenever we are gathered together. Amen.

# *Joy* · DAY TWO

## *God's Great Gift*

**READ ISAIAH 9:2-7**

A child has been born for us . . . and he is named . . . Prince of Peace.
—ISAIAH 9:6 (NRSV)

Last Christmas my mother and I agreed not to give each other Christmas presents. Instead, we decided that we would enjoy the holiday by spending time together, going to church, and visiting with family. Besides saving money, Mother and I decided that we wanted to focus on the true spirit of Christmas.

As Christmas Day neared, it felt slightly odd not to be caught up in the shopping-buying-giving frenzy. Then I felt something stir inside me that was refreshing—and a bit startling. Instead of dwelling on what I could get Mother for Christmas, I reflected on how precious she and other family members are to me. Instead of competing with other shoppers for the best deal at the best price, I smiled more readily and was more available to hold a door open for a stranger. Instead of filling my hours with budget juggling and cost comparisons, I prayed for deeper gratitude and joy at the marvelous, wondrous gift God has given us in Jesus Christ. On Christmas Day, Mother and I agreed that the holiday was our best yet—relaxed, inspiring, and happy.

**Maureen Pratt (California, USA)**

### *Reflection Question*
How would shifting focus from gift-buying and gift-giving to enjoyment of those you love make a difference in your level of joy during Advent?

### *Prayer*
Help us, O God, to celebrate your gift of love by sharing it with others. Amen.

# *Joy* · DAY THREE

## *Joy that Lasts*

**READ LUKE 2:1-20**

The angel said to them, "Do not be afraid; for see—I am bringing you good news of great joy for all the people." —LUKE 2:10 (NRSV)

$A$ small, attractive folder in the mail pictured a young woman with a radiant smile, holding a gift. Below the picture was the word *Joy* in big red letters. Inside the folder were suggestions for gifts that would bring great joy. Advertisers tell us that buying Christmas gifts will bring joy that endures, but we should know better. At best, material gifts bring only fleeting joy.

In contrast, the angel's message brings joy that abides. The Messiah has been born! The shepherds who heard the news went to Bethlehem to see the child. Later the magi, overwhelmed with joy, knelt down and worshiped the Christ child and presented their gifts to him (see Matthew 2:11). The biblical message reminds us that the source of joy is God's love for us. Jesus came to bring us forgiveness and new life. He invites us into his family and assures us of a home in heaven.

Christ brings a genuine joy to all who receive him with a humble heart. Through trusting in Christ, abiding in him, and obeying and serving the Lord, we find joy that lasts a lifetime and beyond.

**Harold Gniewotta (Alberta, Canada)**

### *Reflection Question*
When have you confused temporary joy for lasting joy?

### *Prayer*
Come, Lord Jesus; come to us and to all people. Abide with us, and fill our hearts with love and joy. Amen.

# $\mathcal{Joy}$ · DAY FOUR

## The Bigger Picture

**READ LUKE 1:46-55**

Mary said, "My soul magnifies the Lord, and my spirit rejoices in God my Savior, for he has looked with favor on the lowliness of his servant." —LUKE 1:46-48 (NRSV)

$A$ couple of weeks before her last Christmas, my mother announced during prayer time in worship, "Even though I have been diagnosed with an aggressive form of cancer and the prognosis is not very good, I want everybody to know that nothing can take away the joy of my Christmas!" Her courageous words are etched in my memory.

Reading Mary's *Magnificat* each year reminds me that no matter what happens, our lives are part of a bigger picture. Pregnant and unmarried, Mary would have to make a long, uncomfortable trek to Bethlehem on a donkey's back and finally give birth to her son in a barn. Yet after the angel's words, Mary sang—because she knew God was doing something. In spite of her situation, she realized that she was privileged to be part of a larger movement of God's mercy from generation to generation.

Claiming Mary's spirituality as well as my mom's would mean that no matter what happens to us, we can sing. When we keep our eyes on God, nothing can steal the joy of Christmas.

**Stephen P. West (Alabama, USA)**

### Reflection Question
When have you experienced the joy of Christmas that went deeper than your troubles?

### Prayer
Gracious Lord, even when we are aware of life's struggles during the holidays, may we find that they are indeed holy days. Let nothing distract us from the joy that the Incarnation brings. In Jesus' name. Amen.

## *The Best News*

**READ ROMANS 10:4-17**

The angel said . . . "Don't be afraid! I am here with good news . . . which will bring great joy to all the people. This very day . . . your Savior was born—Christ, the Lord!" —LUKE 2:10-11 (GNT)

During the Advent season, in our house, family members take turns reading aloud our church's annual Advent devotional booklet. This is part of our daily dinner routine. We then share our thoughts and close in prayer.

In Luke's account of Jesus' birth, we read about an angel who announced, "Don't be afraid." I, like the shepherds, would certainly need this reassurance. "I am here with good news," the angel continued. Not only is this good news, it's the best news ever. My Savior was born! Even if I were the only person on the face of the earth, God loved me enough to give me my own Savior. The angel also mentioned "great joy"—and certainly joy is the best word to describe such pure happiness and elation. And this joy is for all the people of the world.

Our challenge is to be an announcing angel for everyone within our reach. With God's help, each of us can carry this joyful message by inviting a friend, neighbor, or loved one to church; by taking a tin of cookies to a shut-in; by calling someone we haven't talked to in a long time; or by buying coffee or a meal for a homeless person. We have the best news that has ever been proclaimed: "Your Savior, your Christ, your Lord has been born!"

**Christine Kalmbach (Texas, USA)**

### *Reflection Question*
How can you share the good news of Jesus Christ in a tangible way this week?

### *Prayer*
God, help us to take the best message ever to everyone we meet. In Jesus' name we pray. Amen.

# *Joy* · DAY SIX

## *Come to Christmas*

**READ ISAIAH 40:3-5**

"See, I am sending my messenger ahead of you, who will prepare your way; the voice of one crying out in the wilderness: "Prepare the way of the Lord."" —MARK 1:2-3 (NRSV)

Christmas garlands and plastic ornaments caught my eye as I walked into the department store. The door was sprayed with fake snow. Shoppers were busy sorting through bins of holiday cards and gift wrap. Young children were pushing their way to the middle of the store to catch a glimpse of Santa Claus. Shopping baskets were filled with packages, candies, and decorations. I could sense the excitement as people rushed in to find the perfect presents for their families and friends.

For a moment, I felt caught up in the frenzy of activity that surrounded me. Then I heard a voice over the store intercom: "Daniel, please come to Christmas." The announcement was a request for an employee to come to the Christmas section of the store, but the message I heard was simply, "Come to Christmas."

As I frantically tried to keep pace with the Christmas season, I heard these words as God saying to me, "Stop your busyness. It is time to prepare for the coming of Christ." What a bold and unexpected message! It was a reminder of the joy, hope, and expectation of Advent: "Come to Christmas."

**Dale Rust Waymack (Tennessee, USA)**

### *Reflection Question*
How do you cut through the frenzy of the season in order to cultivate an expectant heart for the coming of Christ?

### *Prayer*
Loving God, when we are busy with Christmas, thank you for reminders of your Son's presence. Amen.

# FOURTH WEEK OF ADVENT
## *Peace*

## INTRODUCTION

*True lovers of peace are those who, in all their sufferings upon earth, remain at peace in mind and body for the love of Jesus Christ.*

—FRANCIS OF ASSISI

We all know that life is not easy and that peace can be difficult to come by. For many people, heightened anxieties are as much a part of this season as Christmas trees and roast turkey. Yet the writers of this week's meditations remind us that God is present even in the midst of trying situations.

Waiting and keeping vigil can help us slow down enough and be quiet enough to sense God's peace breaking through the chaos. We may be the ones called upon to share a gentle touch and an encouraging word to another who is anxious. Our very home can offer a haven of peace to our families and to visitors.

Year round, whether during Advent or not, Philippians 4:6-7 reminds us of where our peace is found: "Do not worry about anything, but in everything by prayer and supplication with thanksgiving let your requests be made known to God. And the peace of God, which surpasses all understanding, will guard your hearts and your minds in Christ Jesus."

## *God's Presence*

### READ ACTS 16:25-34

Jacob said, "How awesome is this place! This is none other than the house of God." —GENESIS 28:17 (NIV)

Christmastime is my favorite time of the year. Garlands of lights twinkle on the Christmas tree and in all my neighbors' windows. The scent of pine mingles with the scent of sweet-potato pie and freshly baked bread. Hopeful carols and hymns ring through the air. I love our family tradition of placing the little wooden figure of the Christ child in the creche on Christmas Eve, lighting a candle, and singing lullabies.

As I watch the golden light on the ceiling, I am aware that beyond all the hustle and bustle, the true spirit of the season is waiting. In silence and solitude, in quiet times with family and friends, and in worship, we focus on Christ and find the true spirit of Christmas.

God patiently calls me to go beyond just making our surroundings beautiful for Christmas. God calls me to make sure our home becomes a replica of that humble stable—the birthplace of peace, loving-kindness, healing—the birthplace of the living presence of God.

**Deborah A. Bennett (Illinois, USA)**

### *Reflection Question*

How can you help make your home be a place of peacefulness this season?

### *Prayer*

Dear God, be reborn in our hearts this Christmas season. Be reborn in our homes. Reveal to us your living presence. Amen.

## *Message of Peace*

**READ JOHN 1:9-14**

Blessed be the God . . . of all consolation, who consoles us in all our affliction, so that we may be able to console those who are in any affliction with the consolation with which we ourselves are consoled by God. —2 CORINTHIANS 1:3-4 (NRSV)

$A$ few days before Christmas, I had an emotional visit with the family of a patient who was near death. My shift as chaplain was over, but for some reason, I decided to walk back through the emergency unit. I noticed Jennie sitting on her bed, crying, in great pain.

She was in her twenties, and after years of alcohol abuse she had taken her last drink the day before. She had given up. "I have ruined my life; my family hates me; I have no reason to live. Oh God!" she said. I held Jennie's hand and said to her, "Your decision to quit was very difficult and courageous. God loves you and sees you as a person of high value, with unique and special gifts." I continued, "I struggled with alcohol too. I have sat where you sit now. Years from now, you will be able to assure someone else, 'With God's help, you can get through this pain. I did.'"

Peace soon came over Jennie's face, and she lay down to rest. Through the Holy Spirit, God became flesh at Christmas. And God becomes flesh again in us whenever we share with others the comfort we have received from our Creator.

**Dan Nelson (North Carolina, USA)**

### *Reflection Question*
When have you brought a message of peace to another through a gentle touch and word of encouragement?

### *Prayer*
O God, help us be Christ in the flesh for someone in a time of need. In Jesus' name we pray. Amen.

## *Peace of God*

READ MATTHEW 11:28-30

Do not be anxious about anything, but in every situation, by prayer and petition, with thanksgiving, present your requests to God.
—PHILIPPIANS 4:6 (NIV)

The Christmas season is a beautiful time of year, but my anxiety increases as I scramble to buy gifts for loved ones, plan family celebrations, and attend special church services. This anxiety leads to a lack of cheerfulness, and sometimes a sense of depression. However, the apostle Paul wrote, "Do not be anxious about anything."

Why do we have anxieties? Because we live our lives as if we are on our own, forgetting that we belong to God. We forget that our struggles have been lifted through the life, death, resurrection, and ascension of our Lord, Jesus Christ. We fail to focus steadfastly on the Savior.

Listen to these words: "Your Savior was born—Christ the Lord! . . . peace on earth to those with whom he is pleased!" (Luke 2:11, 14 GNT). These words invite us to experience the "peace of God, which transcends all understanding" (Phil. 4:7) during this beautiful and celebrated season.

**Sherry B. Martin (South Carolina, USA)**

### *Reflection Question*
How is prayer a part of your antianxiety strategy this Advent season?

### *Prayer*
Thank you, God, for calming our anxieties. We rejoice in the unselfish and glorious gift of life that is ours through the birth of your son, Jesus Christ. Amen.

# *Peace* · DAY FOUR

## *When Things Go Wrong*

**READ MATTHEW 1:18-25**

All things work together for good for those who love God.
—ROMANS 8:28 (NRSV)

Sometimes life seems completely wrong. A situation we find ourselves in, the turn a job has taken, even relationships with people we thought we knew and loved go wrong. We may ask ourselves, *Why is this happening? What did we do to deserve this?*

Joseph must have wondered the same thing. He had been awaiting his marriage to Mary, and now he found himself betrayed by his fiancée. But Joseph was a man of grace and decided to quietly divorce Mary. We do not know how long Joseph wrestled with this decision or how long he searched for the best way to handle the situation. Probably Mary had thought saying yes to God would be a blessing, and probably Joseph had dreamed of a very different future. Then God's role in all this was revealed to Joseph through a heavenly messenger. How different the story might have been if Joseph had refused to hear the truth!

Romans 8:28 promises us that all things work for good for those who love God. Often it does not seem that way. Nursing an old injury may keep us from accepting the truth. This Advent season is the perfect time to release these old hurts and accept the gifts of love and grace, peace and mercy that await us when we receive the miracle of God's greatest gift.

**Susan Engle (Kentucky, USA)**

### *Reflection Question*
What old hurts do you need to release in order to make more room for God's peace?

### *Prayer*
Holy God, give us eyes to see and ears to hear so we may sense the work you are doing in our lives. Amen.

## *A Quiet Vigil*

### READ MATTHEW 1:18-2:12

God is in heaven, and you upon earth; therefore let your words be few. —ECCLESIASTES 5:2 (NRSV)

Ecclesiastes was a wisdom teacher from the Old Testament, yet his words strike me as sound Advent advice. Advent is a season of waiting and vigil, a time for pondering matters of heaven and earth. Waiting suggests that now is not the time for talk.

The Incarnation itself is a concept more mysterious than explicable—the Word made flesh, the redemption of matter by spirit. Candlelight and "Silent Night" can leave a deeper impression than theological statements. A lack of speechmaking marks Matthew's story of Jesus' birth. At the manger, the humans hardly speak. Angels do, dreams do. Mary and Joseph do not. An exception is the fearful, treacherous Herod: When he speaks to the wise men, he deceives. In the Christmas story, heavenly images—a Bethlehem star, the angelic chorus—communicate more deeply than human speech. I love that about Advent.

We are invited to gaze up at the sky, the same sky that guided the magi, and ponder amazing things in our hearts, as did Mary—things beyond words. With Advent, God forged a new link, a rejuvenating relationship between a weary earth and eternal heaven.

**Ray Waddle (Connecticut, USA)**

### *Reflection Question*
How can I make silence and meditation part of my Advent?

### *Prayer*
Thank you, O God, for the wisdom and renewal we find in silence. Amen.

# $\mathscr{Peace}$ · DAY SIX

## *Waiting in Faith*

**READ PSALM 40:1-5**

I waited patiently for the LORD; he inclined to me and heard my cry.
—PSALM 40:1 (NRSV)

$A$dvent is a time of waiting. I have known waiting. It became a way of life when my children were young. I have experienced the waiting that results in the joyous birth of a healthy child. I have sat by the side of a hospital bed waiting for the results of a CAT scan on a three-year-old child. I have peered anxiously through windows as darkness came and snow squalls increased as I waited for the safe return of newly-licensed drivers. I have cried in anguish through the night, waiting for God's peace to come so I could accept an unacceptable wrong done to my children. I have waited, and it has never been easy.

In a much more profound way, the world waited for Christ. God became human and entered into our world. Because of Christ's birth and life, our waiting takes on new meaning. The birth of a child is the opportunity to share the good news with another generation. Illness is an avenue to draw close to the love and mercy of God. Fear turns to faith that peers through windows on dismal nights, believing that God is faithful. And nights of anguish can teach us that all things can work for good because we love God and God loves us.

**Kathy A. Rohloff (Vermont, USA)**

### *Reflection Question*
When has a time of waiting turned into a time of peace, as you placed your trust in God?

### *Prayer*
Dear Lord, help us to wait in faith, believing that you are with us in every circumstance. May we see you more clearly in these times. Amen.

# SUNDAY AFTER
## *Christmas*

## INTRODUCTION

*Holy living moves us to recognize and claim that God's activity in the world is important, but it is not dependent on any of us individually. God's work requires moments to slow down enough to engage in praise that rocks the depth of our souls. Working hard to bring God's justice, we sometimes overlook our souls and lose our wonder and praise. Both holiness and wholeness are in jeopardy when we put our trust in our own doing rather than in God's presence and activity.*

—JORETTA L. MARSHALL

The meditations for this week challenge us to keep the spirit of Christmas alive all year round. In our culture, we experience such a build-up to Christmas; we may feel a kind of letdown after Christmas Day. However, we can look at the new prayer practices we've experienced during Advent and the challenges to reach out to others as only the beginning of how God may continue to move in and through us.

As you move through Christmas to Epiphany, keep the daily devotional practice that you've maintained during Advent. Resources such as *The Upper Room* daily devotional guide can help you to continue to pray and read scripture regularly. If you've met with a small group during Advent, make plans to begin another study early in the new year.

In the days before a new year begins . . . pray, rest, begin again. Continue to look for the light—on all days and in all seasons.

# CHRISTMAS EVE

## *Many Gifts, One Spirit*

READ ACTS 2:1-13

Beloved, since God loved us so much, we also ought to love one another. —1 JOHN 4:11 (NRSV)

Our first Christmas at Africa University in Zimbabwe, we missed the seasonal changes that herald Christmas back home; even more, we missed our family. It dawned on me that we were not alone in yearning for familiar faces and the warmth of familial love. At least ten different nations were represented in the university student body that year, and virtually none of the students from other countries could go home for the holidays.

Then the Spirit gave me an idea: Invite all the students staying on campus to our home for Christmas Eve dinner. We invited each to bring a dish from their native land. What a feast, and what an amazing celebration we experienced! After dinner, one by one, the students shared a favorite Christmas tradition and taught us, in their various languages, a song that celebrated Jesus' birth. We sang in many tongues, but we were one in the Spirit.

That year, we celebrated Pentecost at Christmas. It must have been similar for those from many nations crowded into Jerusalem at the first Pentecost. The wind of the Spirit whirled around them, filling them with awe as they heard the story of Jesus' life, his crucifixion, and his resurrection. Believers discovered a new family in Christ—and the Spirit still calls each of us to help build that community of love.

**Paul W. Chilcote (Ohio, USA)**

### *Reflection Question*
What is your most memorable Christmas?

### *Prayer*
Spirit of God, fill each of us afresh. In every person we encounter may we find our brother or our sister. Amen.

# CHRISTMAS DAY

## *Waking to Christmas*

READ LUKE 2:8-20

Jesus said, "Peace I leave with you; my peace I give to you. I do not give to you as the world gives." —JOHN 14:27 (NRSV)

Early Christmas morning, I awaken. In the quiet darkness, I take a deep breath and realize that all the days of preparation and frantic busyness have come to an end. This day we celebrate the baby who has been born to us. This baby brings hope and the promise of peace to our world.

On this morning, I think of the earth awakening in quiet darkness, and I pray for the peace proclaimed by the angel—God's peace, a gift to the earth and its people. On this holy day, may all people know peace. May wars and hostilities between nations, cultures, and religions be brought to an end. May troubled, lonely hearts be filled with God's healing presence. May families in conflict be led to reconciliation and love. May anxious, busy minds and spirits be quiet and open enough to receive God's gift of peace. Glory to God in the highest heaven, and on earth, peace among all people, between cultures, within families, and inside my own heart.

**Beth A. Richardson (Tennessee, USA)**

### *Reflection Question*
What is your Christmas prayer for the world and for your own heart?

### *Prayer*
Loving God, thank you for the gift of Jesus, Hope of the World, Bringer of Love, Maker of Peace. Open my heart and the hearts of all people to the Christ child's priceless gift of peace. Amen.

# CHRISTMAS SUNDAY

## *After Christmas*

**READ ESTHER 9:18-23**

If you offer your food to the hungry and satisfy the needs of the afflicted, then your light shall rise in the darkness. —ISAIAH 58:10 (NRSV)

Esther's people set aside two days of celebration that would later become the Festival of Purim. They marked the moment when they were delivered from their enemies, when their sorrow was turned into gladness and their mourning into holiday. They gave presents and food to one another, including the poor. No one was left out of the celebration.

But I wonder how the poor felt when the party was over. Did God's people choose to continue looking after them, or did everything go back to the usual, and the poor remain the poor—out there, on their own?

At times the plight of the poor comes into the spotlight in national or international emergencies, and practical giving increases sharply as people respond with what they have. But the media circus moves on, or the celebration ends and the holidays are over—and the needs of the poor slip out of our view. The stuff of our daily life preoccupies us. Yet scripture tells us that responding to the needs of the poor is to be part of serving God all through the year.

**Susan Hibbins (Lincolnshire, England)**

### *Reflection Question*

How can giving to the needs of the poor remain a practice for you, long after Christmas is over?

### *Prayer*

Lord Jesus, help us to make the needs of others a daily priority and work to relieve suffering. Help us to see your face in the needy and reach out to them as if we are reaching out to you. Amen.

# LIGHT OF LIGHTS
## *Small-Group Guide*

Included here are five meeting outlines for your small-group gathering each of the Sundays of Advent, including the Sunday after Christmas. Read the week's meditations in preparation for each group meeting, which will include lighting the Advent wreath, a brief check-in, discussion of the week's readings, and a weekly prayer practice.

**Prior to Session One:** Distribute books with instructions to read the devotions for First Week of Advent: Hope.

# SESSION ONE: HOPE

### *Materials or Supplies Needed*
Advent wreath
Candle lighter
Bible
Paper and pens

### *Lighting the Advent Wreath*
Talk about the Advent wreath you'll be using each week (see "About Advent" and "About the Advent Wreath" in the Introduction to this book).

On the first Sunday of Advent, light one of the purple candles. *Leader says:* This candle represents the hope that the coming of Christ brings to the world.

### *Opening Prayer* (Read aloud)
O Hope,
aperture of God's expansive view;
prism through which all true Light breaks,
illuminating paths and patterns,
ways and wanderers.
Refract our shortsightedness
that we may look to the East with distance vision
and find our Advent way.
Come, O Hope,
focus our blurred
and distracted sight
that we might see clearly the One who is coming.
Amen.

Sing or read the words to a hymn or Christmas song together.

### *Check-In*
Allow a brief (1- or 2-minute) time for each person to say how the week has been.

### Share & Discuss

Open the discussion with insights from the meditations this week and the word for the week.

- Which meditation spoke to you the most this week? Why?
- How did the readings speak to you about the word for this week, *Hope*?
- What is your prayer for this week?

### Advent Prayer Practice: Writing Prayers

Pass out paper and pens to each person.

*Leader says:* Each week of Advent we will be experiencing a different prayer practice. We will always start with reading one of the scripture passages that was featured in the meditations we read this past week. Today I will read from Ephesians 3:14-21, which was used in meditation entitled "The Sound of Hope." I will read this passage twice. Listen prayerfully. Our prayer practice today will be to write our prayers. After I read the scripture twice, we will have some time to write our own prayers to God, which can be based on the scripture for today, but they do not have to be.

*(Leader slowly reads scripture twice.)*

### Writing Prayers

Allow 10-15 minutes for each participant to write a prayer based on the scripture or other personal matters.

### Sharing/Debriefing Prayer Practice

Those who wish to may read their prayers aloud.

### Closing Hymn or Prayer

# SESSION TWO: LOVE

## Materials or Supplies Needed

Advent wreath
Candle lighter
Bible

## Lighting the Advent Wreath

On the second Sunday of Advent, light two candles—first, the candle from last week, and then another purple candle.

*Leader says*: This candle represents the love of God, demonstrated by sending Christ into the world.

## Opening Prayer *(Read aloud)*

May we choose love, Lord.
May we choose love when faced with retaliation,
love when tempted by deception,
love when addressing poverty,
love when speaking to our neighbors,
love when lured by bad choices.
In all the things we do, in all the words we say, in all the places we go,
may we always choose love.
Amen.

Sing or read the words to a hymn or Christmas song together.

## Check-In

Allow a brief (1- or 2-minute) time for each person to say how the week has been.

## Share & Discuss

Open the discussion with insights from the meditations this week and from the word for the week.

- Which meditation spoke to you the most this week? Why?
- How did the readings speak to you about the word for this week, *Love*?
- What is your prayer for this week?

### Advent Prayer Practice: Intercessory Prayer

*Leader says*: Each week of Advent, we will try out a different prayer practice together. We will always start with reading one of the scripture passages that was featured in the meditations we read this past week. Today, we will read from Isaiah 61:1-3, which was used in meditation entitled "A Record of Tears."

Our theme for the week is Love. One of the most powerful ways we can show our love for others is to pray for them. So, after the reading of the scripture, we will have a time of silent intercessory prayer and then a time of spoken prayer. I will let you know when it's time for spoken prayers by praying aloud. We'll close by saying the Lord's Prayer together.

*(Leader slowly reads scripture twice, then asks these questions aloud for thought during the silence:* Who or what situation came to your mind during the reading today? Who has asked for prayers recently? What situation in your local community needs your prayers today? What world issue is on your heart today?*)*

### Silence (2-3 minutes)

After a time of silence, invite others to offer their spoken prayers for those who wish to pray aloud. End the time of prayer by saying the Lord's Prayer together.

### Sharing/Debriefing Prayer Practice

Those who wish may share their experience with intercessory prayer.

### Closing Hymn or Prayer

# SESSION THREE: JOY

## *Materials or Supplies Needed*

Advent wreath
Candle lighter
Bible
Pens
Markers, colored pencils, or crayons
Unlined paper

## *Lighting the Advent Wreath*

On the third Sunday of Advent, light three candles—the previous two candles in the order they were originally lit, then the rose-colored candle.

*Leader says*: This candle represents the joy of anticipating the coming of Christ.

## *Opening Prayer* (*Read aloud*)

Loving God,
Help me be the face of joy to someone who might be struggling today. If I am facing struggles of my own, gently guide my thoughts toward gratitude, that I may rejoice always in you.
Amen.

Sing or read the words to a hymn or Christmas song together.

## *Check-In*

Allow a brief (1- or 2-minute) time for each person to say how the week has been.

## *Share & Discuss*

Open the discussion with insights from the meditations this week and from the word for the week.

- Which meditation spoke to you the most this week? Why?
- How did the readings speak to you about the word for this week, *Joy*?
- What is your prayer for this week?

### Advent Prayer Practice: Doodle Prayers

Pass out markers, colored pencils, or crayons and unlined paper to each person.

*Leader says*: Each week of Advent we have been experiencing a different prayer practice. We always start with reading one of the scripture passages that were featured in the meditations we read this past week. Today I will read from Isaiah 9:2, 6-7, which was used in meditation entitled "God's Great Gift." I will read the passage twice. Listen prayerfully. Our prayer practice today will be creating Doodle Prayers.

We can speak to God using more than words—we can doodle pictures, and this can be prayer for us. After I read the scripture, write out a word from the scripture that speaks to you. Highlight or circle the word or words that stand out for you. Do the words suggest any visual images for you? If so, draw those near the verse. If not, just use colors to doodle designs around the word. Write questions to God you may have about the verse.

*(Leader slowly reads scripture twice.)*

### Silence (5-7 minutes)

### Sharing/Debriefing Prayer Practice

Those who wish to may share their doodle prayers. (For more information on this prayer practice, see *Praying in Color: Drawing a New Path to God* by Sybil MacBeth).

### Closing Hymn or Prayer

# SESSION FOUR: PEACE

### *Materials or Supplies Needed*

Advent wreath
Candle lighter
Bible

### *Lighting the Advent Wreath*

On the fourth Sunday of Advent, light the previous three candles in order, plus the final purple candle.

*Leader says*: This candle represents the peace Christ brings to the world.

### *Opening Prayer* (Read aloud)

Lord,
Make me an instrument of your peace. Help me to be a compelling witness to the truth that the Prince of Peace is active in this world. Use me as a part of your revealing evidence, everywhere I go and through all that I am.
Amen.

Sing or read the words to a hymn or Christmas song together.

### *Check-In*

Allow a brief (1- or 2-minute) time for each person to say how the week has been.

### *Share & Discuss*

Open the discussion with insights from the meditations this week and from the word for the week.

- Which meditation spoke to you the most this week? Why?
- How did the readings speak to you about the word for this week, *Peace*?
- What is your prayer for this week?

### *Advent Prayer Practice: Silence*

*Leader says*: Each week of Advent we have been experiencing a different prayer practice. We always start with reading one of the scripture passages that were featured in the meditations we read this past week. Today I will read from Matthew 1:18-25, which was used in meditation entitled "A Quiet Vigil." Our prayer practice today will be silence.

(Silence may be new or even uncomfortable for some people in the group, so the leader should take some time to reassure the group that silence is a practice that not everyone will love but it is something that everyone can try. Note that it is a good way to exercise the "listening" rather than "speaking" part of prayer.)

Silence Before and After Reading Scripture: Before starting to read the scripture, allow the group a few moments of silence to quiet themselves, breathing deeply, asking God for a listening heart as the scripture is read. Read the scripture twice. Then set a time—three to five minutes is good—to be silent in God's presence. Instruct participants to meditate on scripture or just enjoy God's presence and not to be surprised if their mind wanders to other things.

After the silence, close by saying "Amen."

### Sharing/Debriefing Prayer Practice

What was the silence like? Were you uncomfortable? Is it a practice you would like to try more often?

### Closing Hymn or Prayer

# SESSION FIVE: CHRISTMAS

### Materials or Supplies Needed
Advent wreath
Candle lighter
Bible
Pens
Paper or index cards

### Lighting the Advent Wreath
On the Sunday after Christmas, all five candles are lit in order, including the white one in the center.

*Leader says*: This candle represents our celebration at the arrival of Christ.

### Opening Prayer *(Read aloud)*
Always-present God,
all the preparations for Christmas are finished,
the presents opened,
the dinner eaten,
the guests have left.
What now?
Help us not to forget You,
as things return to "normal."
Help us to look for you every day.
Help us to look for your needy ones
and to share the hope, love, joy, and peace
that You have so freely shared with us.
Help us to keep looking for the Light.
Amen.

Sing or read the words to a hymn or Christmas song together.

### Check-In
Allow a brief (1- or 2-minute) time for each person to say how the week has been.

### Share & Discuss

Open the discussion with insights from the meditations this week and from the word for the week.

- Which meditation spoke to you the most this week? Why?
- How did the readings speak to you about Christmas this week?
- What is your prayer for this week?

### Advent Prayer Practice: Listening to Scripture for an "Action Item"

*Leader says*: Each week of Advent we have been experiencing a different prayer practice. I hope that these practices of prayer have opened up new ways of praying for you. Today I will read from Isaiah 58:6-9, which was used in the meditation entitled "After Christmas." I will read the passage twice. Listen prayerfully. Our prayer practice today will be to listen for an action item. Pray before I read the scripture that you will be open to how God may be leading you to do something this week, something that requires action.

*(Leader slowly reads scripture twice.)*

Has God brought someone to mind to whom you can show kindness today? Perhaps a random act of kindness for someone you don't even know? An action you need to take in your community? Write it down—then, act on it.

### Silence (3-5 minutes)

### Sharing/Debriefing Prayer Practice

Those who wish to may share their action item.

### Closing Hymn or Prayer

# NOTES

## INTRODUCTION

Opening quote from *Simply Wait: Cultivating Stillness in the Season of Advent* by Pamela C. Hawkins. Copyright © 2007 by Pamela C. Hawkins. Used with permission of Upper Room Books.

## FIRST WEEK OF ADVENT: HOPE

Introduction opening quote from *Rhythm & Fire: Experiencing the Holy in Community and Solitude* edited by Jerry P. Haas and Cynthia Langston Kirk. Copyright © 2008 by Upper Room Books. Used with permission.

"Looking for Jesus" first appeared in *The Upper Room* Daily Devotional Guide in the November/December 2012 issue, under the title "Christmas Day." Copyright © 2012 The Upper Room. Used with permission.

"The Sound of Hope" first appeared in *The Upper Room* Daily Devotional Guide in the November/December 2011 issue, under the title "Christmas Day." Copyright © 2011 The Upper Room. Used with permission.

"Leaning Toward the Light" first appeared in *The Upper Room* Daily Devotional Guide in the March/April 2009 issue. Copyright © 2012 The Upper Room. Used with permission.

"Offering Hope to the Hurting" first appeared in *The Upper Room* Daily Devotional Guide in the November/December 2007 issue, under the title "Beyond Social Boundaries." Copyright © 2007 The Upper Room. Used with permission.

"Hope in the Darkness" first appeared in *The Upper Room* Daily Devotional Guide in the November/December 2007 issue. Copyright

## SECOND WEEK OF ADVENT: LOVE

# THIRD WEEK OF ADVENT: JOY

Introduction opening quote from *A Pilgrim's Almanac: Reflections for Each Day of the Year* by Edward Hays (Ave Maria Press, 1989), 196.

"Time Together" first appeared in *The Upper Room* Daily Devotional Guide in the November/December 2012 issue. Copyright © 2012 The Upper Room. Used with permission.

"God's Great Gift" first appeared in *The Upper Room* Daily Devotional Guide in the November/December 2009 issue. Copyright © 2009 The Upper Room. Used with permission.

"Joy That Lasts" first appeared in *The Upper Room* Daily Devotional Guide in the November/December 2005 issue. Copyright © 2005 The Upper Room. Used with permission.

"The Bigger Picture" first appeared in *The Upper Room* Daily Devotional Guide in the November/December 2011 issue, under the title "3rd Sunday of Advent." Copyright © 2011 The Upper Room. Used with permission.

"The Best News" first appeared in *The Upper Room* Daily Devotional Guide in the November/December 2009 issue. Copyright © 2009 The Upper Room. Used with permission.

"Come to Christmas" first appeared in *The Upper Room* Daily Devotional Guide in the November/December 1998 issue. Copyright © 1998 The Upper Room. Used with permission.

# FOURTH WEEK OF ADVENT: PEACE

Introduction opening quote from "The Admonitions of Francis" from *The Riches of Simplicity: Selected Writings of Francis and Clare*, edited by Keith Beasley-Topliffe. Copyright ©1998 by Upper Room Books. Used with permission.

"God's Presence" first appeared in *The Upper Room* Daily Devotional Guide in the November/December 2002 issue. Copyright © 2002 The Upper Room. Used with permission.

"Message of Peace" first appeared in *The Upper Room* Daily Devotional Guide in the November/December 2012 issue, under the title "4th Sunday of Advent." Copyright © 2012 The Upper Room. Used with permission.

"Peace of God" first appeared in *The Upper Room* Daily Devotional Guide in the November/December 2007 issue. Copyright © 2007 The Upper Room. Used with permission.

"When Things Go Wrong" first appeared in *The Upper Room* Daily Devotional Guide in the November/December 2012 issue. Copyright © 2012 The Upper Room. Used with permission.

"A Quiet Vigil" first appeared in *The Upper Room* Daily Devotional Guide in the November/December 2005 issue. Copyright © 2005 The Upper Room. Used with permission.

"Waiting in Faith" first appeared in *The Upper Room* Daily Devotional Guide in the November/December 2004 issue. Copyright © 2004 The Upper Room. Used with permission.

## SUNDAY AFTER CHRISTMAS

Introduction opening quote from "Greater Wholeness, Deeper Holiness" by Joretta L. Marshall in *The Upper Room Disciplines 2010: A Book of Daily Devotions.* Copyright ©2009 by Upper Room Books. Used with permission.

"Many Gifts, One Spirit" first appeared in *The Upper Room* Daily Devotional Guide in the November/December 2011 issue. Copyright © 2011 The Upper Room. Used with permission.

"Waking to Christmas" first appeared in *The Upper Room* Daily Devotional Guide in the November/December 2007 issue. Copyright

## SMALL-GROUP GUIDE

### Session One: Hope

### Session Two: Love

### Session Three: Joy

### Session Four: Peace